Scaly & Spiky Animals

Teddy Borth

Abdo
ANIMAL SKINS
Kids

abdopublishing.com

Published by Abdo Kids, a division of ABDO, PO Box 398166, Minneapolis, Minnesota 55439.
Copyright © 2017 by Abdo Consulting Group, Inc. International copyrights reserved in all countries.
No part of this book may be reproduced in any form without written permission from the publisher.

Printed in the United States of America, North Mankato, Minnesota.

052016

092016

 THIS BOOK CONTAINS
RECYCLED MATERIALS

Photo Credits: iStock, Shutterstock

Production Contributors: Teddy Borth, Jennie Forsberg, Grace Hansen

Design Contributors: Candice Keimig, Dorothy Toth

Cataloging-in-Publication Data

Names: Borth, Teddy, author.

Title: Scaly & spiky animals / by Teddy Borth.

Other titles: Scaly and spiky animals

Description: Minneapolis, MN : Abdo Kids, [2017] | Series: Animal skins |
    Includes bibliographical references and index.

Identifiers: LCCN 2015959001 | ISBN 9781680804942 (lib. bdg.) |
    ISBN 9781680805505 (ebook) | ISBN 9781680806069 (Read-to-me ebook)

Subjects: LCSH: Body Covering (Anatomy)--Juvenile literature. | Skin--Juvenile
    literature.

Classification: DDC 591.47--dc23

LC record available at http://lccn.loc.gov/2015959001

Table of Contents

Scaly Animals

Animals have skin!

There are many kinds.

Some have scales. They are strong. Some feel **lumpy**. Some feel smooth.

6

armadillo

7

Fish have them.

They are **slick**.

salmon

A snake has them.

They help it move.

python

Alligators have them.

They feel like leather.

alligator

Spiky Animals

Some animals have spikes.

They are sharp.

thorny devil

They can hurt a lot!

They can act as a guard.

porcupine

17

A lionfish has them. It is not easy to eat it. This keeps it safe!

lionfish

19

A hedgehog can roll. It makes a ball. It is a ball of spikes!

hedgehog

21

Other Scaly & Spiky Animals

green iguana

Komodo dragon

io moth caterpillar

tortoise

Glossary

guard
a thing that is meant to keep something safe.

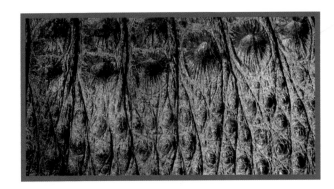

lumpy
rough or choppy.

slick
smooth and glossy; slippery.

Index

abdokids.com

Use this code to log on to abdokids.com and access crafts, games, videos, and more!

Abdo Kids Code:
ASK4942